formations
IMAGES FROM ROCKS

formations

IMAGES FROM ROCKS

Richard Weston

Deukalion Press

In memory of my father, who loved Nature

The author wishes to acknowledge:
Dr Alan Channing and Prof. Dianne Edwards
FRS of the School of Earth, Ocean and Planetary
Sciences at Cardiff University for their interest,
help and advice.
Debbie Campbell of Debris in Cardiff, for
purchases, loans and encouragement.
Brian and Mary Lloyd of Gregory, Botley
and Lloyd in London, for many fine specimens.
Justine Jones and Charlotte Bevan at Crystals,
Cardiff, where it all began.

Published 2007 by Deukalion Press
7 Mill Close
Dinas Powys
CF64 4BR

Tel: +44 29 2051 2719
Email: deukalion@naturallyexclusive.com

A catalogue record for this book is available
from the British Library.

ISBN 978-0-9555113-0-1 (hb)
ISBN 978-0-9555113-0-2 (pb)

Printed by Beacon Printers, Penarth

Contents

Introduction 6
Images from rocks 14
Geological commentary 104
Further reading; picture credits 112

Introduction

This book began unwittingly some three years ago when I happened upon a beautiful ammonite in a shop in one of Cardiff's celebrated arcades. At the time I was experimenting with scanning leaves and flowers into my PC and was tempted to see what might lie beyond the eye's reach in fossils. To my surprise, all that the scanner could capture was a muddy brown shadow of the original. The blame, I suspected, lay not with nature but technology: the scanner cost less than the ammonite, and so I decided to buy the best that Epson could offer. The results were a revelation, and I was captivated.

Since then, thousands of minerals and fossils have been subjected to digital scrutiny, transforming my study, and increasingly entire house, into a cabinet of curiosities. I have learnt to recognise the honey-coloured calcite crystals that occupy the partially-filled segments of that first ammonite, and the golden flecks of pyrite that glitter from an olive green and crimson mudstone matrix, but for me the pleasures remain essentially visual. The ammonite's sinuous chamber walls, mineralised by calcite, could be the model of Hogarth's 'line of beauty' and, like so many such forms in nature, evolved as the optimal solution to a physical problem. In the ammonite's ancestors, the divisions are almost straight; the later curving form gives greater stiffness to the shell wall, which can therefore be both thinner and withstand greater pressures, enabling its occupant to colonise deeper ocean waters.

The development of complex forms through evolution from simple beginnings is a familiar, if still not universally accepted, explanation for life. But unlike the ammonite that stimulated this exploration, all the images in the main body of this book come from the inorganic world of minerals and rocks – and are, therefore, the product of comparatively simple physical and chemical processes (discussed on pp104-111). Despite this, the resulting forms, patterns and colours are often breathtakingly intricate, and impossible to explain in detail with any certainty.

When I showed a print made from part of that first ammonite (*below*) to a colleague in the Welsh School of Architecture at Cardiff University, I described it to him as a terrazzo floor inlaid with brass strips.

Above and right: ammonite fossil, with calcified cell walls and mud-stone infill flecked with pyrite.

'It's obviously Italian, but I don't recognise it. It isn't by Scarpa,[1] is it?', came the response. Faced with the image of jasper (*below*), a neighbour exclaimed: 'Everyone's going to love these. They're made like us, they're organic. You've got cellular life at the bottom and the cosmos at the top.' Such reactions are, in part, a result of our need to tame the unfamiliar by finding meanings through association, and bring to mind Leonardo da Vinci's advice to painters in need of inspiration to 'look at a wall splashed with a number of stains' or – less frequently quoted – at 'stones of various mixed colours' where they will find 'resemblances to a number of landscapes … mountains, rivers, rocks, trees, great plains, valleys, hills'.[2]

Perusing many of the images in this book such visual analogies come irresistibly to mind. Some, such as the agate cloud- and sea-scapes (pp28-33), or paesina stone landscapes (pp16-21) will be almost universally shared, while others, like Shakespeare's 'dragonish' clouds that 'nod unto the world and mock our eyes with air',[3] provoke associations that are altogether more personal.

The digital scanner (or close-up photography[4]) may offer new insights into the beauty of minerals and stone, but appreciation of these qualities is hardly new, as Leonardo's writings and work confirm. He was captivated by the intricate patterns stones may contain, and rendered them in loving detail on the pebbles between the feet of St Anne in the Louvre's *Madonna, Child, St Anne and a Lamb*. And he even devised an ingenious method of recreating them using a bundle of 'small pipes in the manner of goosequills' that yielded 'contours like those in agate'.[5] Such interests were widely shared, and in a radical re-evaluation of Renaissance aesthetics, Hellmut Wohl points out that 'as we read through Renaissance writings on art, it is not uncommon to find greater responsiveness to the aesthetic properties of materials, especially of coloured marble and mosaics, than to works of painting and sculpture'.[6]

What distinguished Leonardo's fascination from that of most of his contemporaries, however, was the passion to describe and understand the processes that gave rise to natural forms, and an ability to suggest interconnections between apparently disparate phenomena. In a celebrated

Above: images from agate and paesina stone.
Below: orbicular jasper

'There are no natural objects out of which more can be learned than stones. For a stone, when it is examined, will be found a mountain in miniature. The fineness of Nature's work is so great, that into a single block, a foot or two in diameter, she can compress as many changes of form and structure, on a small scale, as she needs for her mountains on a large one; and, taking moss for forests, and grains of crystal for crags, the surface of a stone, in the plurality of instances, is more interesting than the surface of an ordinary hill; more fantastic in form, and incomparably richer in colours.' John Ruskin

sheet of drawings depicting turbulent flow, we cannot help but link the helical forms of the upper two studies with his depictions of braided hair, or, thanks to the revelations of telescopes, see in the virtuoso main drawing echoes of the spiralling forms of many galaxies – and to those familiar with the esoteric delights of the fossil world, the interlocking spirals may even recall the inner organisation of a terebratulid brachiopod.

Such analogies may lead to genuine insights, or they may, as with Leonardo's efforts to understand what we would now call the hydrologic cycle by analogy with the flow of blood in our bodies, mislead. The dendrites produced by the diffusion of manganese in solution through limestone (pp74-5), for example, may bear a striking resemblance to plant growth, but are the result of far simpler processes than the genetically controlled formations of leaves and trees. In Hiroshige's *The Sea at Satta in Suruga Province* (*opposite*), the dendritic forms of vegetation also suggest a link to the fractal outline of a breaking wave, which in turn resembles a miniature of the coastline along which it is about to wash. Such suggestions of correspondences across disparate scales and phenomena abound in images from rocks, and in the case of paesina stone are grounded in similarities of formation, the small-scale structures being a result of analogous processes of sedimentation and fracture to those that form large-scale landscapes.

By comparison with biological forms the formation of minerals and stones may be relatively simple, but like everything in nature the results are prodigiously diverse. Nature, as Leonardo observed of plants, is 'so

Above, from top:
Dendritic Lichtenberg figure, formed by 6MeV electrical discharge through an acrylic block (visit www.teslamania.com).
Manganese dendrites growing through limestone.
Turbulence in ocean waters.
Right: Leonardo da Vinci, *Studies of Hydrodynamic Turbulence* (c. 1508-9), pen and ink.

delightful and abundant that there would not be one that resembles another, and not only plants as a whole, but among their branches, leaves and fruit, will not be found one which is precisely like another.'[7] Or, as Ruskin wrote of clouds: 'You may try every other piece of cloud in the heaven, and you will find them every one as perfect, and yet not one in the least like another. … Where Poussin or Claude has three similar masses, nature has fifty pictures, made up each of millions of minor thoughts … all unlike each other except in beauty.'[8] Similarly in mountains, he suggested, 'the multiplicity of form is oceanic'.[9]

The most touching example of this inexhaustible variation is surely the snowflake, and the first scientific attempt to explain its geometry was made by the mathematician and astronomer Johannes Kepler.[10] Lacking the insights of crystallography his task was hopeless, but although we can now readily account for its six-fold symmetry from our understanding of the close-packing of atoms, the snowflake's flatness and all-but-identical elaboration of each arm still elude full explanation.[11]

As a committed Platonist, Kepler believed that regular geometric figures ordered everything in nature, and he would have found today's account of snowflake-formation deeply disturbing, because at its heart lies the recognition of an essential irregularity in the arrangement of the hydrogen atoms in an ice crystal. Snowflakes are products of both order and disorder, and their endless diversity is a response to minute variations in the atmospheric environment in which they form, not the inexorable outworking of an inner architecture.[12]

Above: snowflakes, from a vast collection of photographs first published in 1931 by W. A. Bentley and W. J. Humphreys.
Left: Hiroshige, *The Sea at Satta in Suruga Province*, 1858, woodblock print from the series *Thirty-six Views of Mount Fuji.*

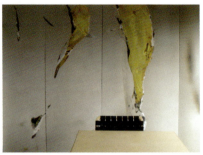

Above: Quartz tip with inclusions used to make image (p63) for linen-covered storage-wall doors.
Below: Hercules Seghers, *Mountain Valley with Four Trees,* etching, c.1630

Commenting on the apparent lack of purpose in a snowflake's shape, Kepler suggested that 'formative reason does not act only for a purpose, but also to adorn. It does not strive to fashion only natural bodies, but is in the habit also of playing with the passing moment, as is shown by many ores from mines.'[13] With minerals the 'passing moment' of their formation may be rather longer, but they still communicate a feeling that nature is at play in creating their purposeless beauty, and, as with snowflakes, the circumstances of growth are just as vital to the eventual form as the underlying crystal structure.

Like artists who go 'fishing for idealities'[14] amongst the variability of nature, many mineral collectors are latter-day Platonists seeking out specimens that conform most closely to an ideal Form. For my purposes, however, more interesting by far are those that have been invaded by impurities, contorted and broken by unimaginable stresses – those, in short, that feel like a life lived. The 'ideal' quartz tip is perfectly clear, clearer than the best glass, whereas the images made from quartz on pages 60-71 are traces of all manner of contamination – by inclusions of gases and water, and of other minerals and elements. Such minerals, and the images they yield, have what Gerard Manley Hopkins extolled as the 'pied beauty' of nature's 'dappled things'.[15] These qualities abound at every scale in nature, but were systematically excluded by classical art in its search for ideal beauty, as Sir Joshua Reynolds made clear in his *Discourses on Art.* The power of art, he declared, lay in discovering, in order to eliminate, 'what is deformed in nature … what is particular and uncommon' so that art could 'rise above all singular forms, local customs, particularities and details of every kind'.[16]

If they affirm anything, the images in this book suggest the pleasures to be found in 'particularities and details'. And in doing so, they point

to the fact, central to the sciences of complexity,[17] that instability and irregularity, not a classical sense of form, are at the heart of natural processes. Amongst European artists a fascination with process rather than form is surprisingly recent. Leonardo is an obvious exception, as is that most 'geological' of artists, Hercules Seghers. In his etching of a *Mountain Valley with Four Trees* we see convoluted, gnarled forms that may have begun in observation of actual landscapes, but are marshalled to conjure up a 'cosmic' vision of creation, not as a finished form but – like this intermediate state of the etching – a work in progress.

As with Leonardo's studies of water, the feeling of form and order emerging from flux lends Seghers' work a certain modernity, linking it, in spirit at least, to Paul Klee, who was amongst the first to assert the primacy of process over form in the making of art. In his *View of a Mountain Sanctuary*, for example, diverse forms – some, like the mountain of the title, readily identifiable, others generically 'natural' or man-made – emerge as disturbances in the field of parallel lines that establish the basic architecture of the picture. Klee collected minerals, but it would be misleading to over-interpret such a picture as being intended to represent the folding and fracturing of sedimentary strata or banded minerals. He did, however, describe his way of working as analogous to that of nature: 'A sense of totality has gradually entered into the artist's conception of the natural object, whether this object be plant, animal, or man', he wrote, enabling 'a new naturalness, the naturalness of the work'.[18]

Above: Paul Klee, *Ansicht eines Berg-Heiligtums* (View of a Mountain Sanctuary), indian ink and watercolour, 1926.
Below: Digitally printed silk for 'Frocks from Rocks', made using images from mica (p54) and calcite (p57).

Klee's vision of a universal process of formation reaches out to Eastern attitudes to nature and reverberates back through the Western Romantic tradition, to which he was deeply indebted: 'In organic life', observed Goethe in his *Botany*, 'nothing is unconnected with the whole, and even if the phenomena appear isolated to us ... it does not prove that they actually are isolated.'[19] This feeling of interconnection recurs in the study of minerals and it is not so surprising, therefore, that one of the nineteenth century's keenest students of biological form, Ernst Haeckel, came to sense in the complex symmetries of 'crystal souls' the elusive unity of organic and inorganic nature.[20]

Such intimations of what the physicist David Bohm[21] has called the 'implicate order' of nature are, for me, amongst the principal satisfactions to be found in contemplating these mineral images. Like the 'profuse strains of unpremeditated art' that delighted Shelley in the song of a skylark, so in many of these formations one may sense something akin to that superlative adjustment of part to part, colour to colour, that Rilke discovered in the paintings of Cézanne: 'It's as if every part were aware of all the others.'[22]

It is now time to confess another, more practical, reason for countless hours spent with scanner and screen. The database of images I was amassing, it gradually dawned on me, constituted a quarry from which could be extracted 'designs' for all manner of digitally manufactured materials, from printed and woven fabrics to rugs and ceramic tiles.

Although the virtues of nature as a model for design were widely ignored during Modernism's embrace of the machine, they were never entirely occluded and, for designers of the second generation such as Alvar Aalto, were a constant source of inspiration. The sinuous cast-glass

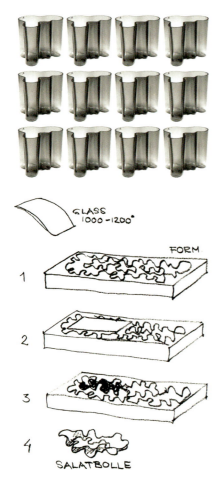

GLASS
1000-1200°

FORM

1

2

3

4

SALATBOLLE

Top: Alvar Aalto, *Savoy Vase*, 1937, manufactured by Artek.
Above: Jørn Utzon, idea for making a sald bowl, c.1950.
Below: 'Rugs from Rocks': digitally woven rug based on a 230 million-year-old fossil coral.

forms of his Savoy vase, for example, are a recognised classic of 'organic' design. They strike many as an echo of the undulating shores of Finland's lakes and, like the lakes, there could be countless appealing variations on this formal theme. The exigencies of mass-production, however, mean that they must be identical, struck from the same mould and lending them, en masse, the unnerving quality of biological clones rather than that 'natural variation' to which Aalto, like Ruskin, aspired.[23]

This difficulty, we may surmise, was in the mind of Jørn Utzon when he proposed a process – not a fixed 'design' – for creating free-form salad bowls. They were to be made by melting sheets of glass over a mould that resembled an exaggeratedly hilly terrain. By varying the sizes of the sheets, and their positions on the mould, the resulting bowls would have the subtle variability of flowers or snowflakes.[24]

Many designers are now pursuing 'emergent' forms using computer software, the products of which can be materialised using a variety of numerically-controlled modelling and milling machines. This work is in its infancy and the results to date, while generically biomorphic, have neither the rigour nor playfulness – in the sense Kepler suggested apropos snowflakes – of natural forms. But these may come in time: relatively simple algorithms have already been devised, for example, to create the artfully variable patterns found on seashells.[25]

My own interests are technologically less ambitious, and use digital processes to replace traditional industrial or craft ones: digital printing in place of silk-screening of fabrics or hand-painting of tiles, or digitally controlled looms that can make unique rugs or woven fabrics. What the scans of minerals and rocks bring to this is a potentially unlimited source of intricate designs to exploit the flexibility of digital production, which makes short-run, even one-off production of a wide range of goods economically feasible.

In a global market based on inequalities between economies and concentration of manufacturing in developing, low-wage countries, flexible digital production may never compete, on cost alone, with mass-

produced goods. The opportunities it is opening up, however, are radical: in place of mass-production and its latest variant, 'mass customisation', we are likely to see a growing individualisation of both production and consumption; in place of global brands spending vast amounts to promote their 'exclusivity', we could have genuinely exclusive goods, custom-made, not just cleverly marketed.

For designers and makers the new global market could offer an almost unlimited range of niches from which to reach customers world-wide. The weightless information of digital designs can travel freely around the Web, while physical production could again be distributed in small-scale units. And in happy counterpoint to these global delights, the digital revolution might help to foster the re-emergence of more locally designed and produced goods that delight in those 'singular forms, local customs, particularities and details' that Joshua Reynolds so despised.

This all too brief prospecting of the near future may seem a long way from the world of minerals, but I can think of few more apt analogues of what may be in prospect as we negotiate new relationships between the global and the local. The images in this book are made from specimens from all over the world – Brazil and Madagascar, India and Russia, Canada and Italy, Australia and South Africa – yet there are rocks and minerals beneath all our feet. These may not be as readily accessible or enticing as those circulating in the global marketplace, but the pleasures of the local, of things particular to place or country, will, I suspect, be increasingly valued in an ever more globalised world.

And so let us end, as we began, with the particular. To mark the United Nations' 'International Year of Planet Earth' in 2008, BBC Wales has commissioned a study for a rug to hang in Broadcasting House, Cardiff. The design, from a beautiful piece of greenschist found on Anglesey, in the most complex geological region in Wales, would look well anywhere. But as an image it feels inescapably particular, distilling the essence of the moist greens, fine grain and bright water of the Welsh landscape, and suggesting new means towards the celebration of locality.

Below: Image from a piece of green-schist found on Anglesey, Wales.

Notes

[1]Carlo Scarpa was a Venetian architect noted for reviving traditional skills.
[2]William Wray, *Leonardo in his own words*. London: 2005, p91.
[3]William Shakespeare, *Antony and Cleopatra*, act 4, sc. 12, l. 2-6.
[4]See, for example, Bill Atkinson, *Within the Stone*, San Francisco: 2004, and Georg Kern, *Stone. Colours and forms of a hidden world*, London: 2005.
[5]Martin Kemp, *Leonardo da Vinci. The Marvellouos Works of Nature and Man*, London: 1981, p343.
[6]Hellmut Wohl, *The Aesthetics of Italian Renaissance Art*, Cambridge: 1999, p153.
[7]William Wray, op. cit., p61.
[8]John Ruskin, *Modern Painters*, 2nd edn., Vol I, pp244 and 249-50.
[9] *Ibid.*, p298.
[10]Johannes Kepler, ed. and tr. by Colin Hardie, *The Six-Cornered Snowflake*, Oxford: 1966
[11]Philip Ball, *The Self-Made Tapestry. Pattern Formation in Nature*, Oxford: 1999, pp121-3.
[12]Lancelot Law Whyte, 'Kepler's Unsolved Problem and the *Facultas Formatrix*' in Kepler, op. cit., pp57-63
[13]*Ibid.*, p33
[14]Ruskin, *Modern Painters*, Vol. I, p336.
[15]'Pied Beauty' in *Gerard Manley Hopkins: Poems and Prose*. Harmondsworth: 1953, p30.
[16]Sir Joshua Reynolds, ed. Robert R. Wark, *Discourses on Art*. New Haven and London: 1997, p44.
[17]See for example Stuart Kauffman, *At Home in the Universe*, London: 1993.
[18]In *The Thinking Eye. The Notebooks of Paul Klee*, Vol. 1, ed. Jürg Spiller, London and New York: 1961, pp.63-7 (orig. pub. 1923).
[19]Quoted in Richard Verdi, *Klee and Nature*, London: 1984, p221.
[20]Olaf Breidback, *Visions of Nature. The Art and Science of Ernst Haeckel*, Munich and London: 2006, pp277-83.
[21]David Bohm, *Wholeness and the Implicate Order*, London: 1980.
[22]Rainer Maria Rilke, tr. Joel Agee. *Letters on Cézanne*. New York: 2002, p.71.
[23]See my *Alvar Aalto*. London: 2005 and John Ruskin. 'The Nature of Gothic' in *Stones of Venice*, Vol II, Ch. VI.
[24]See my *Utzon*. Hellerup: 2002, p348. The method is in fact, impracticable; a bowl using a revised technique is planned by Edition Bløndal.
[25]Hans Meinhardt, *The Algorithmic Beauty of Seashells*, Berlin: 2003.

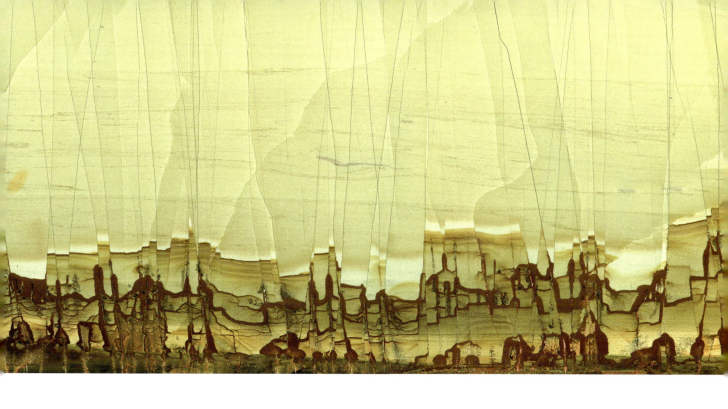

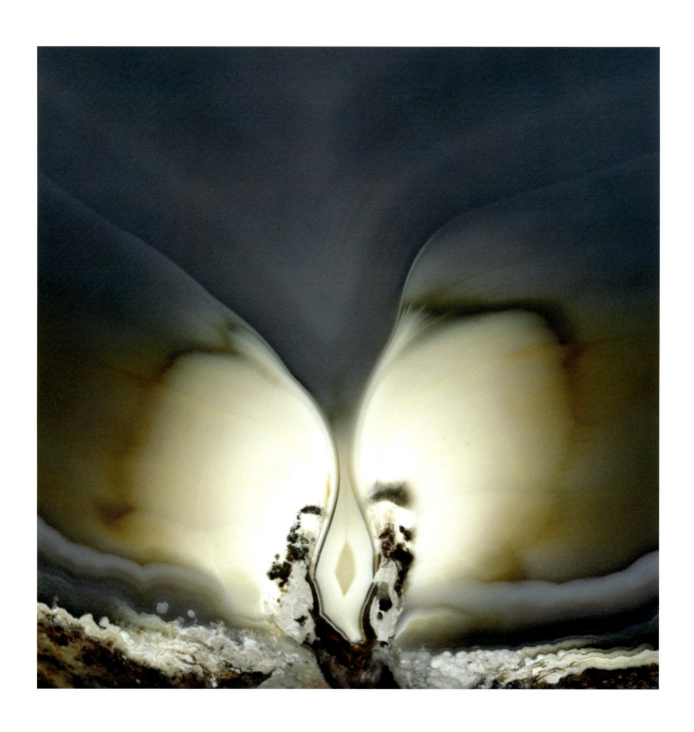

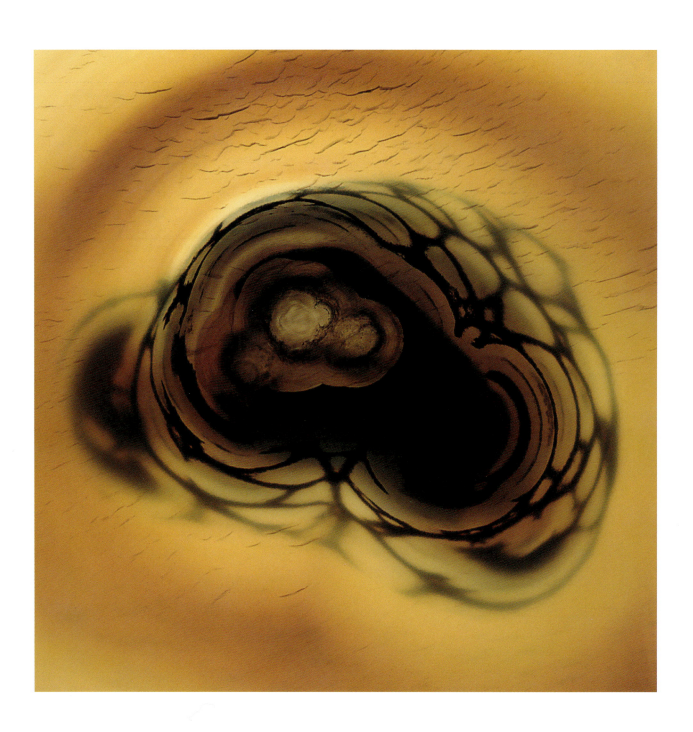

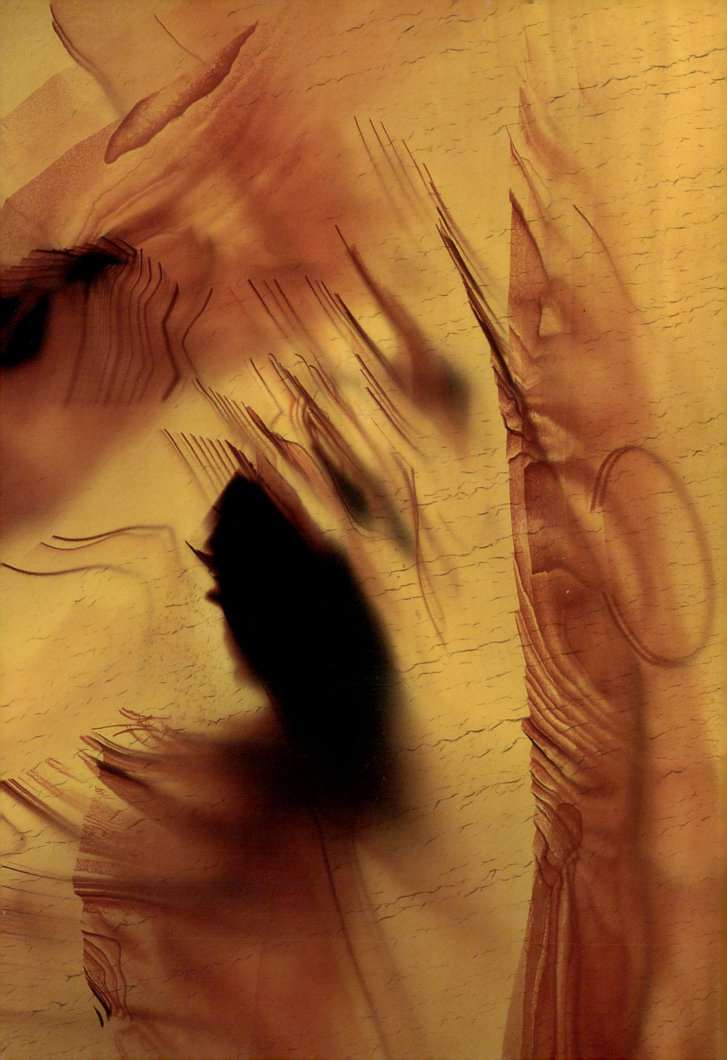

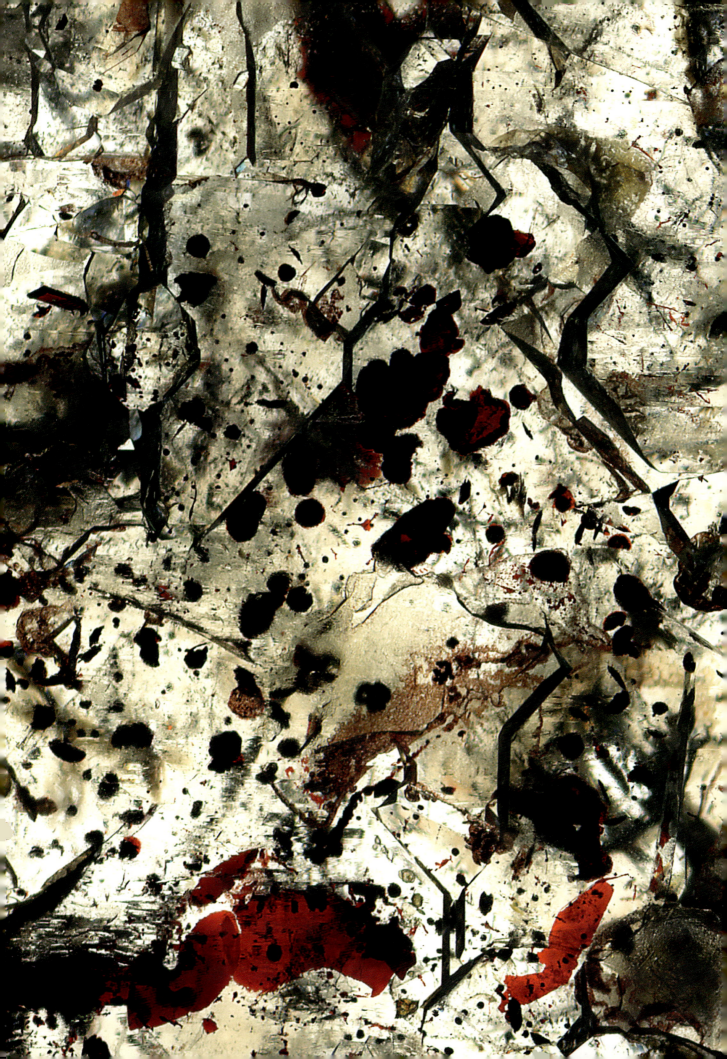

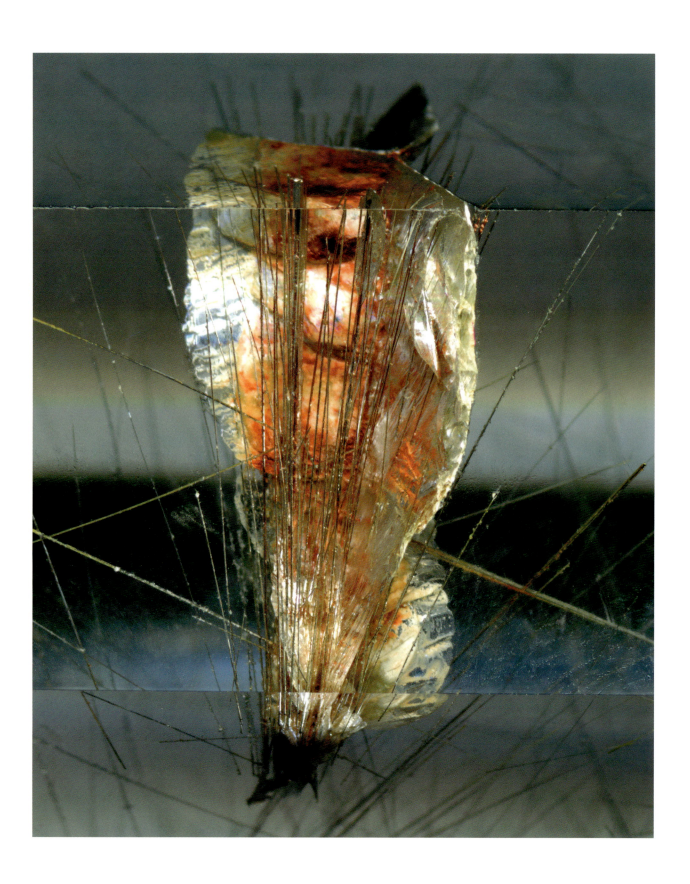

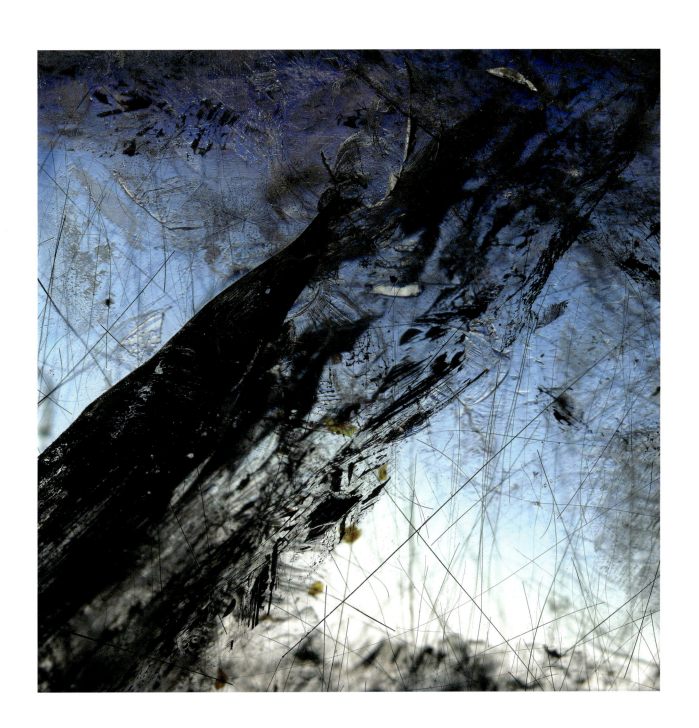

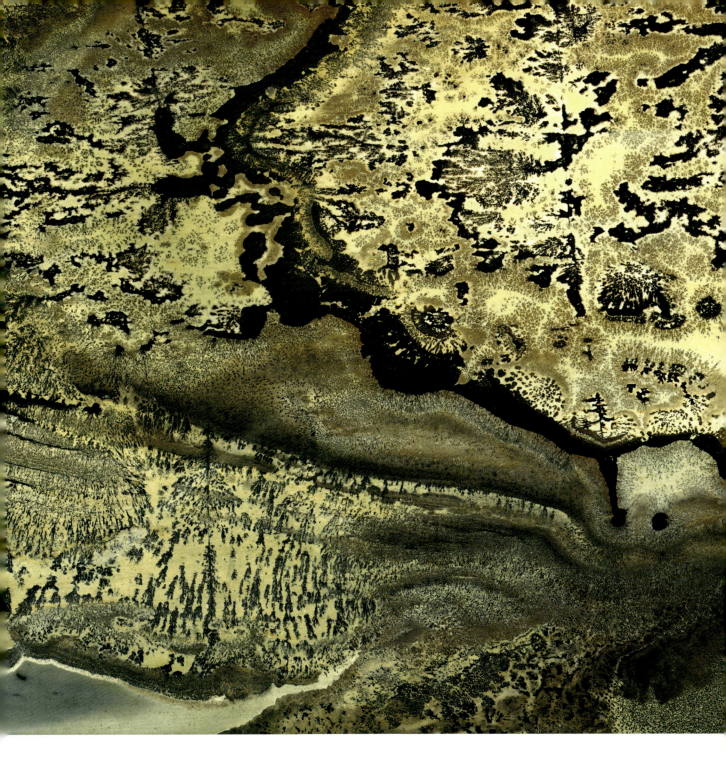

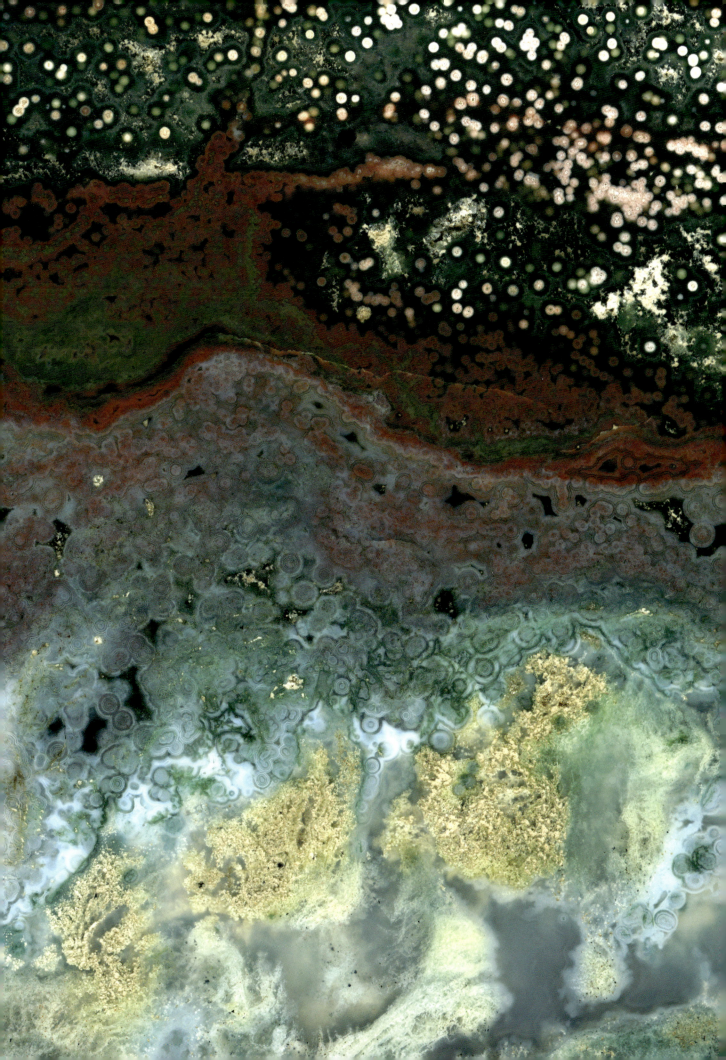

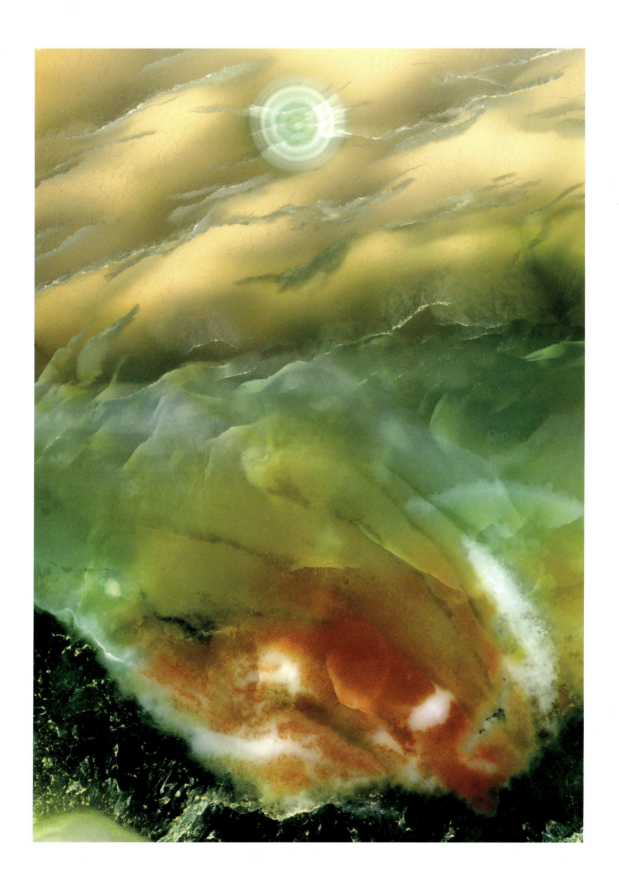

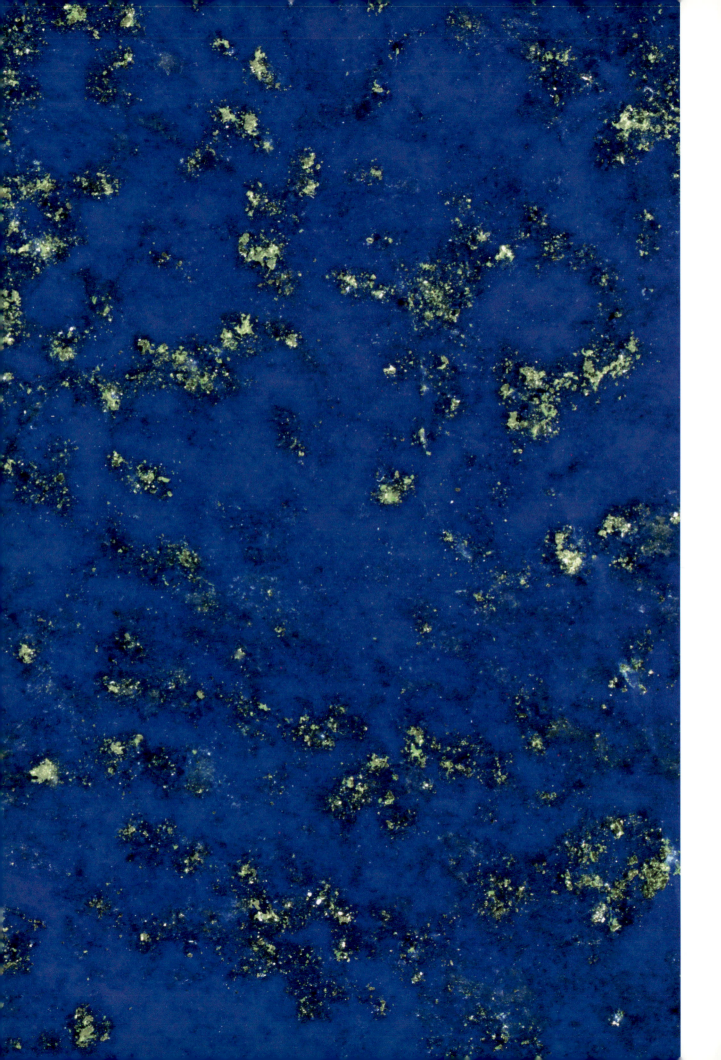

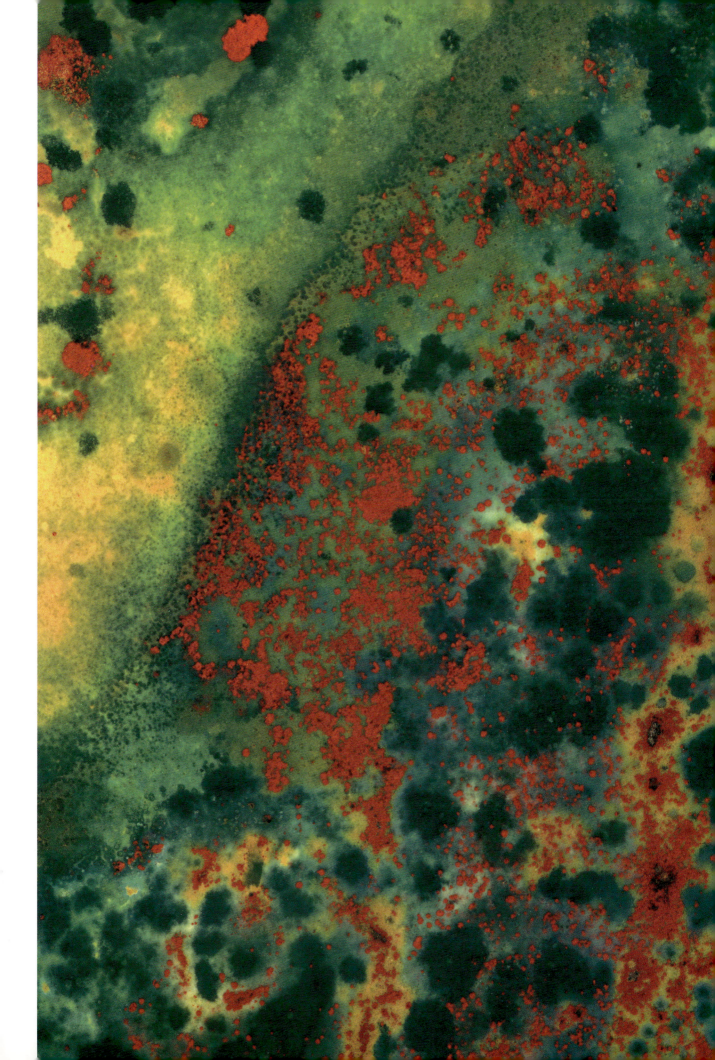

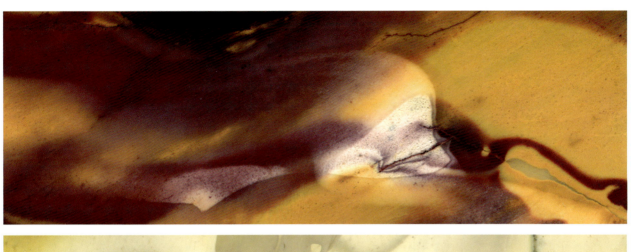

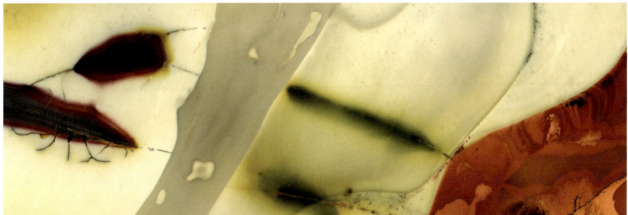

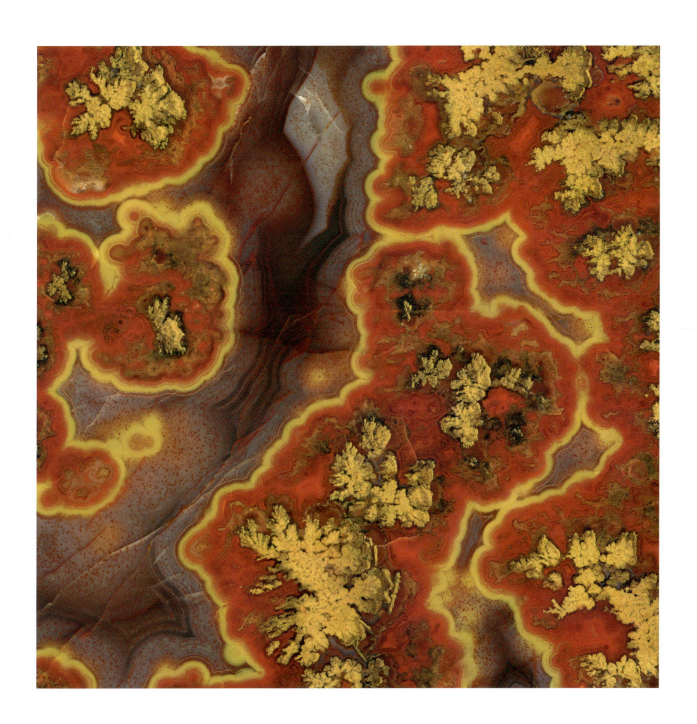

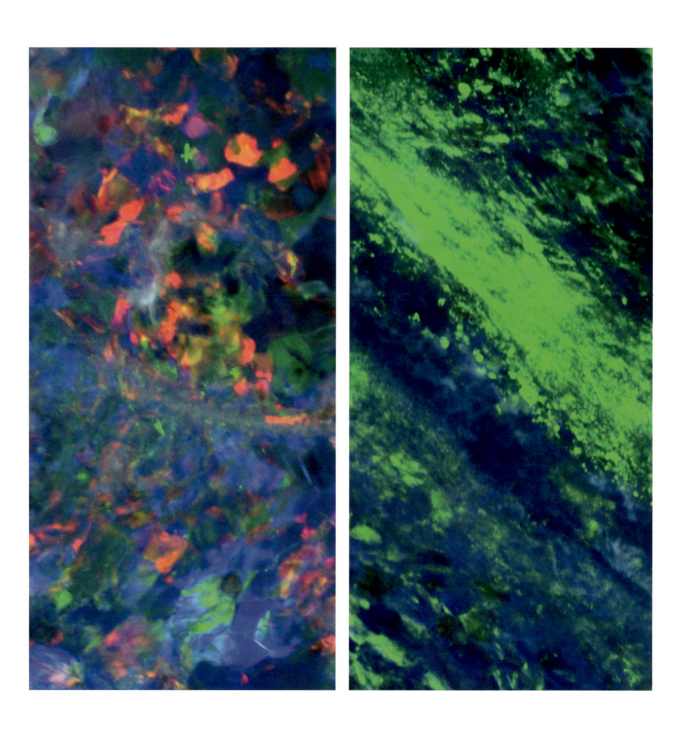

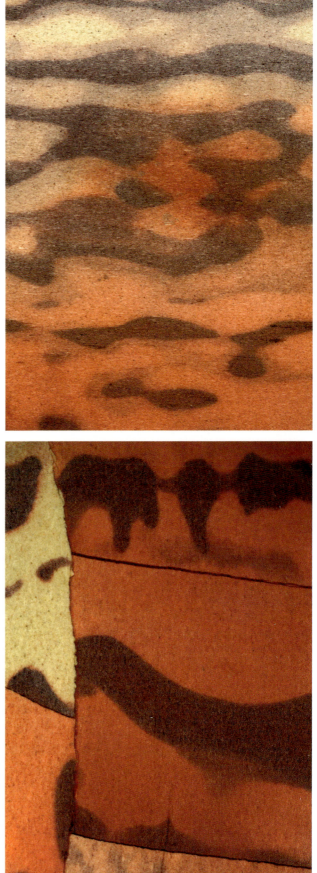

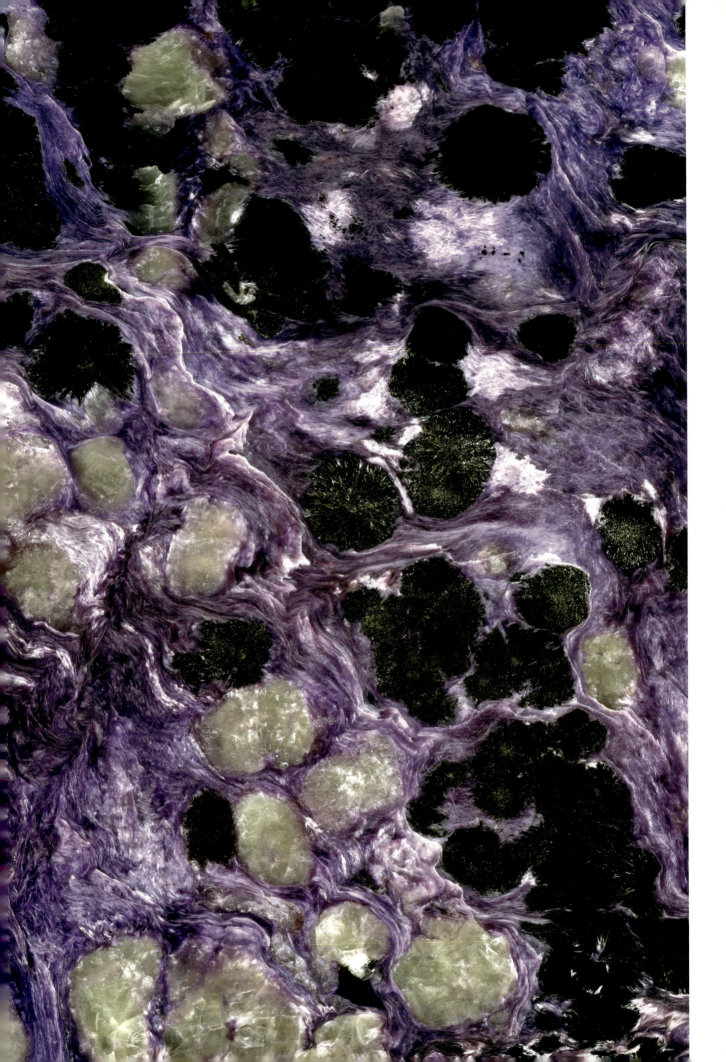

Geological commentary
Alan Channing

Earth is a dynamic planet in a state of constant change. Rocks and minerals are perpetually created, destroyed, transported and re-formed into new generations of rocks and minerals. Geologists use the expression 'the rock cycle' to encompass this grand, planetary-scale tour. Where to start? Earth has a simple basic structure – a solid nickel and iron inner-core, a molten outer-core comprising the same elements, a solid but plastic mantle rich in magnesium and silicon and a relatively thin but rigid crust with oceanic and continental components.

Earth's crust can be divided into about a dozen major plates, the continental plates (like Africa, Europe, Australia and the Americas) which are about 35km thick and separated from one another by oceanic plates (like the Pacific, Atlantic, Indian and Antarctic), with crust about 6km thick. In the process of plate tectonics rafts of cool, rigid crust are driven in a conveyor-belt fashion across the globe. Energy as heat from the core and mantle is convected to Earth's surface, creating bodies of molten rock (magma). Because it is hot and buoyant, this rises to the surface at linear chains of volcanic activity that traverse the centres of the major oceans. At these oceanic-ridges, magma is erupted or intruded into the crust and cools to form solid rock. Later generations of magma are forced up at the ridge, shouldering these rocks aside. Gradually this forces old, cold and therefore dense crust away from the ridges towards the basin margins. Here, the dense crust descends, in the process known as subduction, back towards the mantle as it is forced below thicker and more buoyant continental crust. Slowly, over millions of years, subduction can devour entire oceanic plates, leading to the collision of two continental plates. There, subduction cannot occur as both plates have similar buoyancy:

Image keys (RW)
Each image key gives: the page numbers of the spread; the common name of the mineral; and the magnification of the image on each page (x).
'T' indicates that the specimen has been scanned using transmitted rather than reflected light, and 'inv.' that the colours have been inverted in the computer.

endpapers: crazy lace agate: 10x.
Finely banded lace agates such as the specimen featured on the cover and endpapers are generally found in veins in rocks rather than as nodules formed in air pockets in volcanic lavas.

2: tiger's eye: 10x.
Tiger's eye is generally throught to be formed by the silicification of crocidolite ('blue asbestos'), although this has recently been questioined. It is widely used in the jewellery trade.

14-15: paesina stone; 4x; 2x.
Paesina stone is a fine grained silty limestone with a complex 3-D network of fracture planes through which oxygen-rich groundwater diffuses.

16-17: paesina stone: 4x; 8x.
Groundwater diffusing through paesina stone transports iron from the rock and re-precipitates it in rhythmically repeated bands, creating stunning land- and sea-scapes.

18-19: paesina stone: † 1.5x; l 2.5x; r: 1.5x.
These 'scenes', including part of a specimen of exceptional length, are uncannily reminiscent of the Tuscan landsape and towns around Florence, near where the stone is quarried.

20-21: paesina stone: 4x; 2x.
Cosimo de Medici, a passionate admirer of paesina stone's decorative qualities, commissioned several tables surfaced with numerous pieces of the material.

instead, massive pressures are exerted, forcing up mountain ranges like the Himalaya.

So to the rock cycle: at its heart the rock cycle has a simple tripartite classification into igneous (formed of fire), sedimentary (settled down) and metamorphic (from the Greek 'to change form'). Linking the three corners of this classification are all the processes that form rocks; volcanism, magmatism, sedimentation and metamorphism. At crustal plate margins volcanism and intrusion of magma create igneous rocks. Basalts erupt from the sub-oceanic volcanoes at ocean ridges, while below the ridges the magma chambers cool to form coarse gabbros. Andesitic lavas erupt explosively from volcanic chains above continental subduction zones building mountain ranges like the Andes. Again, below the volcanic landscape, magma bodies cool, forming coarse diorite rocks.

Beyond the crust, Earth's oceans and atmosphere act to destroy rocks, the next step in the rock cycle. Igneous rocks and minerals, created at high temperatures and high pressures deep in the crust, are often inherently unstable in the cold, wet conditions of Earth's surface. They weather chemically, breaking down to their constituent minerals or becoming altered to more stable minerals, such as clays, by hydration. Physical processes are also at work. Ocean waves pound coastal cliffs, glaciers reduce granites to rock flour, and rivers carve vast canyons. The water that provides the common agent of erosion also forms a means of transport for rock particles. Glacial debris from the Himalaya is transported by vast river systems across the continent, eventually to be deposited in deltas and in ocean basins. Particles of sand are driven thousands of miles across deserts by the wind. As the energy available for transport wanes,

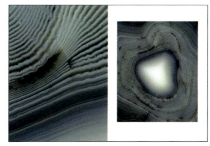

22-23: agate: 12x; 2x.
In this beautiful, fine-grained agate, the almost uniformly coloured bands follow the walls of the vesicle in which they formed – hence the generic term 'wall-banded' to describe it.

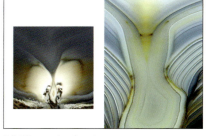

24-25: agate: 8x; 4x.
'Tubes of escape' such as these are a common feature of wall-banded agates, caused by excess liquid material being expelled by internal pressures during formation.

26-27: agate: 5x; 7x.
The level-banded agate in these Oregon 'thunder eggs' is known as onyx, after the Greek word for the human nail, which also appears horizontally-ridged when seen side on.

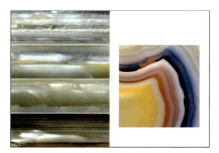

28-29: agate: c.4x; 2x.
These 'sea and sky' formations are typical of level-banded agates and form a striking contrast to the exquisite colours of the wall-banded agate on the right.

30-31: agate: 2x; 3x.
The delicately graded colours of these agates are the result of iron-rich solutes that entered the gel either during formation or after crystallisation.

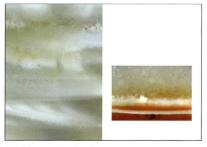

32-33: agate: 5x; 3x.
The banding of the agate on the left has all but disappeared, transforming it into a vivid evocation of a sky. Like so many reds in nature, the colourful 'sunset' on the right comes courtesy of iron.

particles are deposited, forming unconsolidated sand, mud and clay sediments. Over time these build up layer by layer, bed by bed, and form thick sediment sequences. The sediments become progressively buried and transformed by cementation and compaction into solid sedimentary rocks like sandstones and mudstones.

Sedimentary rocks themselves are eroded, potentially time after time, forming and reforming sediments and sedimentary strata. Sediment deposited in the ocean basins hitches a ride atop the oceanic crust, eventually to be transported to subduction zones and into continental collision zones. As oceanic crust and sediments are driven down subduction zones, the fluids within them act to lower the melting point of the overlying continental rock. This generates partial melting and magma formation, creating volcanic activity. In collision zones, the sediments are compressed and heated in the process of metamorphism. Mud rocks and sandstones change to slates and schists. With increasing temperatures and pressures at depth the rocks buried beneath up-thrust mountain ranges become plastic, deform and partially melt to create folded and banded gneisses and granites. The massive mountain ranges once again become intense zones of erosion and the rock cycle commences again.

Volcanism, metamorphism and deep burial in the crust create hot fluids which can dissolve rocks and minerals. These buoyant, element-laden fluids ascend towards the surface, progressively cooling along the way. The dissolved elements they contain become saturated and are forced to precipitate, creating mineral veins and pods within older rocks. Layer upon layer of minerals precipitated as bands within a single vein indicate the changing chemistry of mineralising fluids over time, producing

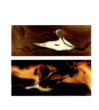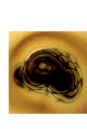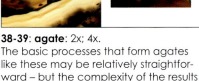

34-35: **agate**: 1.5x; t 6x; b 2x - T.
The banding of the 'fortification' agate on the left shows exquisitely graded colours. The image top right is from a stone that was cut and poished in Victorian England to form a pendant.

36-37: **agate**: 9x - T; 4x - T.
Transmitted light reveals the exceptionally intricate formations of this beautiful specimen from Minas Gerais in Brazil.

38-39: **agate**: 2x; 4x.
The basic processes that form agates like these may be relatively straightforward – but the complexity of the results still feels almost miraculous.

40-41: **agate**: 2.5x - T; 12x - T.
Many of the intricate and fragmented formations in this Brazilian agate defy easy explanation.

42-43: **malachite**: 5x; 3x.
A carbonate of copper, malachite is a secondary mineral formed by the percolation of rainwater into copper ores. It typically shows, as here, a banded radiating, structure.

44-45: **tiger's eye**: 5x; 4x.
Tiger's eye is formed when quartz replaces the cross-fibres of asbestos in crocidolite, although the precise details of its formation are much disputed. It is found primarily in South Africa.

mixed assemblages of metals like gold, silver, pyrite and lead. Where precipitation occurs slowly within open fractures, large perfectly-formed crystals of minerals such as quartz develop.

Each image in this book is a graphical representation of a point within this grand planetary scale cycle frozen in time. Each contains glimpses of this story played out at the scale of molecules to mountains and beyond, at the planetary-scale. Some, such as the paesina stones with which the images begin, look uncannily like 'real' landscapes, and in part this is because of a genuine correspondence between small- and large-scale processes. With many others, similarities of appearance are deceptive. Horizontally-banded agates, for example, might appear to be the product of a simple process of sedimentation, whereas in fact the process is more complex, and far from fully understood.

Agates, which supply more images in this book than any other mineral, are made of chalcedony, a microcrystalline form of quartz, and form in voids within former rocks. Typically the most spectacular examples come from open pockets created by trapped gas bubbles in basalt lavas. Ground water percolating through the basalts dissolves silica and other elements that are transported into the voids via fractures and cracks. Agate structure comprises concentric shells differentiated by colour, which is derived from differences in the orientation of the microscopic fibrous crystals that make up the rock plus variations in trace elements within the crystals. The precise mechanisms of agate formation are still poorly understood. In some instances concentric bands completely line cavity walls and formerly deposited bands. Here it appears that the void in which precipitation was occurring was completely full of silica-rich fluid.

46-47: tourmaline: 20x; 16x.
These images are made from the same piece of schorl (black) tourmaline. The speciment appears jet black, the colours being produced optically only when light strikes at particular angles.

48-49: quartz: 12x - T.
The most various of minerals, quartz can contain inclusions of other minerals (the red is due to hematite), gases and fluids, through which traces of the crystal structure are just visible.

50-51: mica: 3x - T; 8x - T.
Mica cleaves perfectly into paper-thin sheets which, in the absence of other minerals, may be perfectly clear. The (dis)colouration reveals the 60° lattice of the crystal structure

52-53: mica: 3x - T; 6-12x - T.
These patterns result from minerals penetrating the crystal lattice of mica. The sinuous rainbow bands (top right) are diffraction patterns formed between delaminating layers.

54-55: meteorites: 4x; 8x.
The Widmanstätten structure (right) can only form extra-terrestrially as iron meteorites cool slowly in near zero-gravity conditions in space. It is only partially formed in the example on the left.

56-57: calcite: 15x - T; 8x - T.
Calcite is unique in the diversity of its crystal forms. These images, stunning in their subtlety of line and colour, come from a pale blue rhombohedral crystal, skewed to orthogonal in the computer.

58-59: calcite: 7x - T; 8x - T - inv.
Both these images are from pale yellow calcite crystals, digitally skewed to square. The verticals in the right-hand image are traces of the mineral's cleavage planes.

Top: cubic pyrite crystals
Above: Scanning Electron Microscpe image of quartz crystals - the largest is less than 2mm long,

Other agates have stacked bands that appear to be formed horizontally under the influence of gravity. In these examples it appears that only part of the void was fluid-filled allowing silica only to be precipitated below the water level or, alternatively, that a process of sedimentation was active whereby silica particles were precipitated in the fluid and grew to dimensions too large to remain in suspension.

Crystal structure and mineral habit

We are all familiar with metallic cubes of pyrite – so-called 'fool's gold' – or the six-sided quartz crystal with its pyramid-like point. These are two of the strictly limited number of geometric crystal systems which form because the minerals' constituent elements, such as oxygen and silica in quartz, or iron and sulphur in pyrite, can only bond chemically in a few predefined configurations. These create crystal faces, and planes of structural weakness within the crystal lattice known as cleavage planes.

Other minerals have extremely homogeneous structures. Agates formed of chalcedony, a microcrystalline and near-amorphous form of quartz, are structurally identical in all directions and when they fracture produce conchoidal, shell-like surfaces. Mica forms tabular plate-like sheets which separate relatively easily because chemical bonds between elements in adjacent sheet surfaces are far weaker than those within the sheets themselves. Structural weaknesses – lines of cleavage – cross the sheets at 60 degrees to one another and may allow trace elements to migrate along them (see pp5, 50-3). Other crystal shapes include needle-like 'acicular' crystals, (e.g. rutile, pp68-9) and fibrous forms such as asbestos (which may be silicifed to form tiger's eye, pp2, 44-5).

60-61: quartz: 2x; 6x.
Both these images are records of inclusions of minerals, gases and liquids in otherwise clear quartz tips. The r.h. image was scanned against a white background, that on the left with none.

62-63: quartz: 7x - T; t 4x; b 8x
The l.h. image is from an oval-shaped 'palmstone', the others from quartz tips. The colours in the lower r.h. image are both 'real' (eg red hematite) and optically created.

64-65: quartz: 4x; 6x - T.
The l.h. image is from a large citrine (yellow) quartz, rich with inclusions; that on the right from a quartz tip liberally spattered with specks of hematite.

66-67: quartz: 3.5x.
Scanned from one of the earliest quartz tips I bought, I still find it extraordinary to think that the raw materials for this turbulent 'decisive moment' have lain frozen in time for millions of years.

68-69: quartz: 12x; 8x.
The fine 'rods' in the l.h. image are inclusions of rutile (titanium oxide). The r.h. image is a part-enlargement of the previous spread, scanned against a different background.

70-71: quartz: 10x; 6x - T.
The subtly graded 'sky' in the r.h. image is created by internal reflections when the light from the scanner's lamp enters the crystal at a specific angle.

Dendrites

Branching patterns are amongst the most familiar in nature across a wide variety of scales, from plants to the river-drainage system of an entire region. Known generically as dendrites, from the Greek word for tree, they arise in a variety of ways: as the most efficient means of distributing liquids – blood in the body, or water in trees; of gathering flows, as in river-systems – or of dissipating energy, as in electrical discharge through lightning or the Lichtenberg figure illustrated on p8. Dendrites are also examples of the 'fractal' structures that have attracted much attention in the popular scientific literature since they were first described in the 1960s by the mathematician Benoit Mandelbrot.

The classic embodiment of dendritic mineral formation occurs where manganese in solution diffuses into a crack within a rock and reacts with oxygen to create manganese oxide. Dendrite formation begins when an initial manganese oxide particle forms a solid, insoluble and immobile nucleus. Other manganese ions which are diffusing within the fracture are at concentrations too low to allow oxide precipitation. However, when ions encounter the nucleus particle they can precipitate.

The characteristic fractal, branching pattern emerges one particle at a time, as the ions diffuse through the water in which they are dissolved via random paths generated by collisions with the water molecules. Because they 'stick' irreversibly to the growing dendrite, the mineral ions have no opportunity to rearrange themselves into a characteristic, close-packed crystal structure. Known as diffusion-limited aggregation, this somewhat esoteric-sounding process can be readily simulated on computers to yield dendrites strikingly similar to those found in nature.

Above: organic and inorganic processes may lead to similar forms: fern frond and dendrite created by a discharge through a dielectric material.

72-73: **fluorite**: 4x - T - inv.; 5x - T.
Clear when pure, fluorite - like quartz - is most commonly found with impurities and imperfections that give rise to the forms and colours captured here.

74-75: **limestone**: t - 3x; b - 2x; 6x.
The dendrites on these stones are formed by manganese crystals. Top left is a Chinese picture stone (the white disk lower left is a fossil coral), the others are from the Solnhofen quarry in Germany.

76-77: **agate**: 12x - T; **quartz**: 16x.
The foliage-like forms in both these images result from manganese dendrites growing in cracks and - in the case of the 'mocha' agate on the left - between bands.

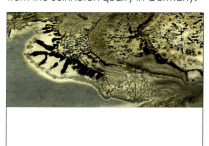

78-79: **limestone**: 2x.
The magnificent 'coastline' of this Chinese picture stone – an oriental version of paesina stone (pp14-21) – is overlain with tiny dendritic growths.

Colour

A multitude of phenomena produce colours in minerals, the most common source being small amounts of metallic elements such as iron, manganese and copper distributed in the crystal lattice. These absorb certain wavelengths of light: iron and manganese in quartz produce the purple of amethyst, and copper in malachite gives green.

Microscopic structural features of crystals also provide colour, as light is scattered or bent. Tiny fibrous crystals within chalcedony – the microcrystalline form of quartz found in agates and jasper - give a milky blue colouration as light breaks into rays, the red component is generally absorbed and the blue reflected. Elements are also incorporated into crystals as inclusions, tiny finely distributed pockets of gas liquid or solid; again these act to scatter light (pp60-73).

Cleavage, the regular arrangement of planes of weakness in a crystal structure is another source of mineral colour. In moonstone and labradorite, for example (pp102-3), closely packed lamellar cleavage surfaces reflect and break up light into its component colours. In opal (pp92-3), the mineral structure is created by microscopic silica spheres: packed in a regular arrangement, these produce a brilliant play of colour as light is reflected and diffracted by the silica particles.

Rock degradation and weathering also provide intricate and subtle colour variation. Rocks containing iron minerals weather to give reds, while unoxidised regions of the same rock retain greens and greys. In Indian paint stone (p95), for instance, cracks within the rock have concentrated the flow of water and hence these sites of oxidation, producing the characteristic red 'brush strokes'.

Dr Alan Channing is a geologist and palaeontologist whose research interests include hot spring ecosystems, the processes by which they become fossilized and the formation of hot spring sedimentary deposits. He combines research with work on public engagement with science in the School of Earth, Ocean and Planetary Sciences at Cardiff University.

80-81: jasper: 2-15x.
The concentric bands and colouration of these spherical orbicules in various jaspers are agate-like: their formation is complex, and far from fully understood.

82-83: jasper: 6x; 1.5x.
Jasper is a microcrystalline form of quartz containing up to 20% impurities, the source of its varied textures and colours. Parts of the lower half of the r.h. image are almost transparent.

84-85: jasper: 3x; 10x
Amongst the 'strange worlds' conjured up by many of these images captured from minerals few, if any, seem to me stranger than that in the r.h. image.

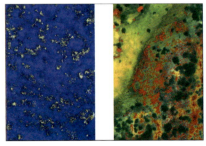

86-87: lapis lazuli: 7x; **bloodstone:** 5x.
Lapis lazuli is the source of the prized pigment ultramarine; here it is peppered with pyrite. Bloodstone or heliotrope is a form of green jasper scattered with blood-red spots of hematite.

88-89: nephrite: 4x; **mookaite:** 1-2x.
The green colour of this Canadian nephrite ('jade') is due to iron. Mookaite, from Australia, is a siliceous rock made of skeletons of Radiolaria (unicellular marine organisms).

90-91: agate: 3x; 2.5x.
The intense red and yellow colours of the r.h. image are the most intense of any agate in my collection – it seems fitting, therefore, that the specimen came from Morocco.

Towards the end of his book *The Ethics of the Dust*, John Ruskin offers this vivid description of the rock cycle.
Left: image from tiger's eye

'Through all the phases of (earth's) transition and dissolution, there seems to be a continual effort to raise itself into a higher state; and a measured gain, through the fierce revulsion and slow renewal of the earth's frame, in beauty, order and permanence. The soft white sediments of the sea draw themselves, in process of time, into smooth knots of sphered symmetry; burdened and strained under increase of pressure, they pass into a nascent marble; scorched by fervent heat, they brighten and blanch into the snowy rock of Paros and Carrara. The dark drift of the inland river, or stagnant slime of inland pool and lake, divides, or resolves itself as it dries, into layers of its several elements; slowly purifying each by the patient withdrawal of it from the anarchy of the mass in which it was mingled. Contracted by increasing drought, till it must shatter into fragments, it infuses continually a finer ichor into the opening veins, and finds in its weakness the first rudiments of a perfect strength. Rent at last, rock from rock, nay, atom from atom, and tormented in lambent fire, it knits, through the fusion, the fibres of a perennial endurance; and, during countless subsequent centuries, declining, or, rather let me say, rising, to repose, finishes the infallible lustre of its crystalline beauty, under harmonies of law which are wholly beneficent, because wholly inexorable.'

92-93: opal: 15x; **rhyolite**: 4.5x.
The colours in opals are caused by rainbow iridescence and tiny amounts of minerals other than silica. Rhyolite is a silica-rich volcanic rock; the type shown here is known as 'Jupiter stone'.

94-95: tiger pebbles: 2.5x; **indian paint stone**: 9x. The 'brushstrokes' of colour on indian paint stone are caused by the migration of trace elements along cracks. The markings on tiger pebbles are less easily accounted for.

96-97: chrysocolla: 3x; 2.5x.
Occurring in the oxidation zone of copper deposits, chrysocolla is frequently found – as in the l.h. image – in association with malachite (see pp42-3).

98-99: copper ore: 7x.
The striations on the copper are a product of the polishing process; the grey-white 'clouds' are small particles of quartz.

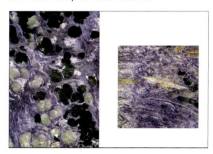

100-101: charoite: 3x; 2.5x.
Discovered as recently as the 1970s in the banks of the River Chara in Siberia, charoite has a distinctive purple colour and wonderfully fluid-looking structure.

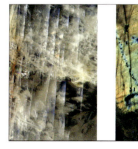

102-103: moonstone: 4x; **labradorite**: 3x.
Both moonstone and labradorite are varieties of feldspar and flash with spectral 'film' colours.

111

Suggestions for further reading

Richard Fortey, *The Earth. An Intimate History*, London: HarperCollins, 2004.

Marcia Bjornerud, *Reading the Rocks. The Autobiography of the Earth*, Cambridge, Mass: Basic Books, 2006.

Ronald Louis Bonewitz, *Rock and Gem*, London: Dorling Kindersley, 2005.

Walter Schumann, *Rocks, Minerals and Gemstones*, London: HarperCollins, 1992.

Philip Ball, *The Self-Made Tapestry. Pattern Formation in Nature*, Oxford: Oxford University Press, 1999.

Bill Atkinson, *Within the Stone*, San Francisco: Browntrout, 2004.

Georg Kern, *Stone. Colours and forms of a hidden world*, London: New Holland, 2005.

Richard Weston, *Materials, Form and Architecture*, London: Laurence King, 2004.

Picture credits

p8: Lichtenberg figure: Bert Hickman, Stoneridge Engineering (visit www.teslamania.com for fascinating products and images).

Aerial view of turbulent water: NASA (public domain).

Leonardo drawing: The Royal Collection © 2006 Her Majesty Queen Elizabeth II.

p9: Snowflakes: from *Snow Crystals* by W. A. Bentley and W. J. Humphreys, pub. by McGraw Hill, 1931.

Hiroshige woodcut: The British Museum.

p10: Etching by Hercules Seghers: The British Museum

p11: Watercolour by Paul Klee: Sprengel Museum Hannover; photograph by Michael Herling/Aline Gwose.

p12: Drawing of salad bowl: Jørn Utzon/Edition Bløndal

p13: Greenschist: specimen, collection of the National Museum Wales; scanned image by the author.

p108: SEM image of quartz, Prof. Paul Wright, Cardiff University.

p109: dielectric 'fern': source unknown.

All other pictures by the author.

Website

Visit **www.naturallyexclusive.com** to view an ever-growing library of images from rocks and a wide range of digitally manufactured goods, including prints, fabrics and ceramics.